# My First Pony

KINGFISHER

Kingfisher Publications Plc,
New Penderel House,
283–288 High Holborn,
London WC1V 7HZ
www.kingfisherpub.com

First published by Kingfisher
Publications Plc 2006

10 9 8 7 6 5 4 3 2 1
1TS/0706/SNPLFG/CLSN(CLSN)/140MA/C

ISBN-13: 978 0 7534 1460 6
ISBN-10: 0 7534 1460 0



A CIP catalogue record for this book is available from the British Library.

Printed in China

Consultant: Elwyn Hartley Edwards
Editor: Russell Mclean
Designers: Poppy Jenkins, Jack Clucas
Photographer: Matthew Roberts
Picture research manager: Cee Weston-Baker
Senior production controller: Lindsey Scott
DTP co-ordinator: Catherine Hibbert

Ponies supplied and produced by Justine Armstrong-Small BHSAI, pictured with Zin Zan (Champion Working Hunter, Horse of the Year Show 2004; Champion Lightweight Working Hunter, Royal Windsor Horse Show 2005).

Clothing and equipment supplied by Cuddly Ponies, Dublin Clothing and Roma (www.dublinclothing.com).

Roma

Dublin
Ride. Life. Style.

The Cuddly Ponies Club

# My First Pony Care

Judith Draper

KINGFISHER

# Contents

# You and your pony

Having a pony of your own is great fun. If there is space to keep him at home, you can spend lots of time together and will quickly become friends. Ponies take a lot of looking after, every day of the year, so you will need the help of an older person.

It is important to know how to handle ponies confidently. Learn how to do this at a riding school before you have a pony of your own.

# Perfect partners

Your pony should be the right size for you, not too big or too small. If you are a beginner, look for an older pony that is well trained and well behaved.

You do not have to own a pony to become a good rider. Riding lots of different ponies at a school is an excellent way of learning to ride well.

If you don't have a stable and paddock, you can keep your pony at someone else's stables. This is called 'livery'.

# Breeds

Many different breeds make good riding ponies. They come in all sorts of shapes and sizes, from the little Welsh Mountain pony to the Connemara, which is strong enough to carry a grown-up.

## Connemara

The beautiful Connemara comes from Ireland. It jumps well and makes a wonderful pony for shows and competitions.

The Caspian pony is the oldest breed of horse or pony. It stands no more than 12 hands high, but is strong enough to be ridden by children.

The Morgan horse is a light breed from the USA. It is spirited but has a kind nature. It is used for both riding and driving.

## Welsh Section A

The handsome Welsh Mountain pony is also called the Section A. It is the smaller cousin of the gentle Welsh pony, or Section B. Both make perfect riding ponies.

Icelandic horses are small, strong and confident on their feet. Sometimes they use an unusual, very fast running-walk called the 'tolt'.

### Safety first!

For young riders, a first pony must have a kind nature and be easy to handle.

# Grass and hay

A pony has a small stomach that cannot manage large meals. To stay healthy, he needs to eat small amounts of foods called 'roughage' right through the day. Grass, hay, haylage and chaff are all types of roughage.

## Tasty foods

A pony can spend up to 20 hours a day moving from place to place in search of the tastiest grasses and herbs. There is more goodness in grass in the spring and summer than in the autumn and winter.

## Safety first!

If a pony eats too much grass in the spring, he may get a painful disease called laminitis. This can damage the bones in his feet.

A pony eats more slowly if you feed him from a haynet. This is good for his stomach and stops him getting bored.

Tie the haynet quite high up the stable wall, so that your pony cannot get his foot stuck in it.

## Hay

Hay is made from specially grown long grasses that are cut from meadows in summer. The cut grass is dried out and then made into bundles called 'bales'. Hay provides roughage for stabled ponies. It is also used for ponies that live outside during winter, when there is little goodness in the grass.

Top tip

### Soaking

If your pony is very sensitive to the tiny germs in hay, soak it in water (for no more than 30 minutes) before feeding.

Feed bowls and water buckets should be kept clean. Scrub them regularly with fresh water.

## Mix and measure

Write down all the ingredients in your pony's feed and how much he has at each meal. Measure his food carefully and mix it up well.

sugar beet

feed scoop

# Hard feed

When ponies are ridden every day, they usually need extra food, called 'hard feed', to give them more energy. Pony cubes, coarse mixes, oats, barley, maize and sugar beet are all types of hard feed.

Sliced apples and carrots taste good and contain vitamins and minerals. They are called 'succulents'.

Top tip

## Safe bucket

Stand your pony's water bucket in an old rubber tyre to stop him from knocking it over.

# Clean water

Ponies must always have a supply of fresh water. In the stable, water can be given in a bucket. Check the bucket often to see if it needs topping up. In the field, use a special trough or a container such as a plastic bin.

Water buckets are usually made of plastic or rubber.

## Cool down

Never give your pony a long, cold drink straight after riding him. It could give him an illness called colic. Walk him about until he is cool and has stopped puffing.

Top tip

## Clean feet

Remember to pick out your pony's feet before you lead him out of the stable. This helps to keep the yard clean.

Except in very bad weather, the top half of a stable door is left open to give your pony plenty of fresh air.

Always walk in the yard. Never run about.

American barn stables are found in many countries. They are very useful when the weather is bad.

# Stables

There are two main types of stable. Outdoor stables are built in a row or around an open space called the stable yard. Stables can also be inside a much larger building. This is known as the American barn system.

When you go through a door with your pony, lead him in a straight line so he does not bang himself.

A stable yard can get messy very quickly! Everyone needs to help keep it neat and tidy.

Light switches are placed where a pony cannot reach them with his teeth.

Drains have strong metal covers. They are kept clean all year round.

Stable doors have two bolts – one at the top and another at the bottom.

Stable windows are made of extra strong glass. Metal bars protect the glass.

# Mucking out

If your pony is stabled, muck out his bed every day. Take droppings and wet bedding to the muck heap. If your pony is left standing on dirty bedding, he could get an infection in his feet called thrush.

1 Use a fork or shovel to pick up all the droppings and place them in a wheelbarrow.

2 Fork all the dry bedding against the stable walls or, even better, into a clean corner.

3 Sweep the floor clean of any more droppings and damp straw. Add these to the wheelbarrow.

4 Pile up fresh straw against the stable walls and cover it with some of the old straw. Use the rest to make a deep bed in the middle of the stable.

### Safety first!

After you have mucked out, never leave tools such as forks and shovels in the stable in case your pony hurts himself.

## Skipping out

Remove droppings from your pony's bed as often as possible during the day. Use a fork or shovel and a container called a 'skip'. Clearing away droppings regularly helps keep the pony clean and makes mucking out in the morning easier.

### Safety first!

If your pony is in the stable when you are mucking out or using a skip, always tie him up.

1 When you skip out a woodchip bed, use a special woodchip fork to lift the droppings into the skip.

2 Use the fork to shake up and level off the bed. Make sure that the whole floor is covered with bedding.

3 Woodchips are put down in the same way as straw, piled up at the sides to protect a pony's legs from knocks and cold draughts.

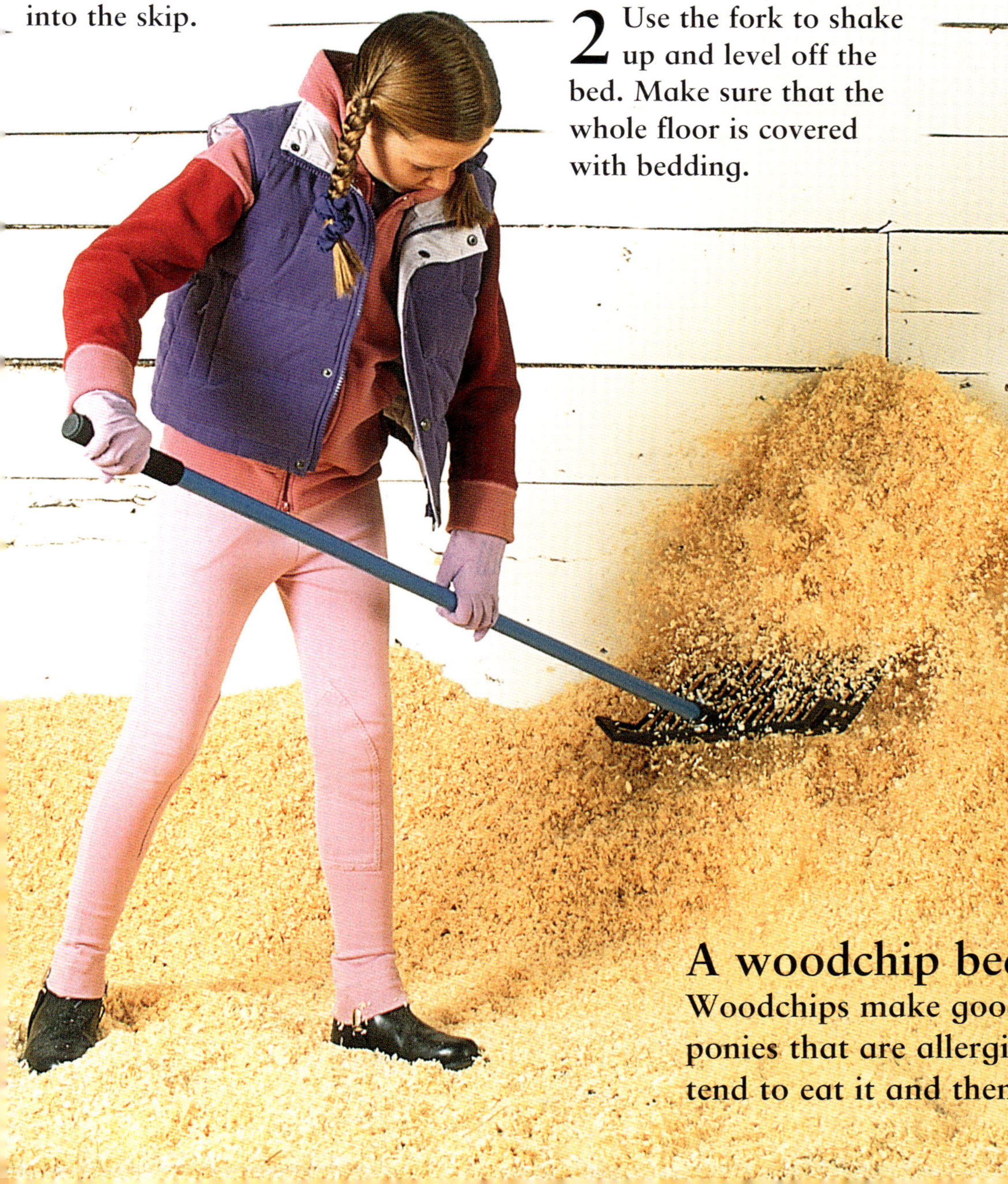

## A woodchip bed

Woodchips make good stable bedding for ponies that are allergic to straw or that tend to eat it and then become fat.

# Handling a pony

It is very important to handle a pony correctly and safely. You must learn how to ask him to move about in his stable, how to pick up his feet for cleaning, and how to lead him.

Top tip

## Mounting

A well-trained pony should stand still while you mount. If your pony fidgets, someone must stand at his head.

It is usual to lead a pony from the left side. But practise leading from the right too, in case you ever need to.

Hold both reins in your right hand, just below the pony's head. Hold the buckle-end of the reins with your left hand so that neither you nor the pony can trip over them.

## Safety first!

Before leading your pony, run the stirrup irons up the leathers to stop them flapping and scaring him.

The metal tying-up ring is fixed tightly to the wall. A loop of baler twine or string is tied to it.

To stop your pony undoing the knot with his teeth, pass the end of the lead rope through the loop.

Top tip

## Safe string

Tie the rope to the string, not the ring. If the pony moves suddenly, the string will break and stop him from panicking.

## In the stable

Tie up your pony whenever you are working in his stable – mucking out, grooming or tacking up, for example. Ask an adult to show you how to tie a quick-release knot in the lead rope.

# In the field

Ponies are happiest when they are turned out in a field for at least part of the day. This is more natural than living in a stable. In winter, your pony may need to wear a weatherproof rug to keep him warm and dry.

A sturdy field shelter will give your pony a place where he can escape from very wet or very hot weather.

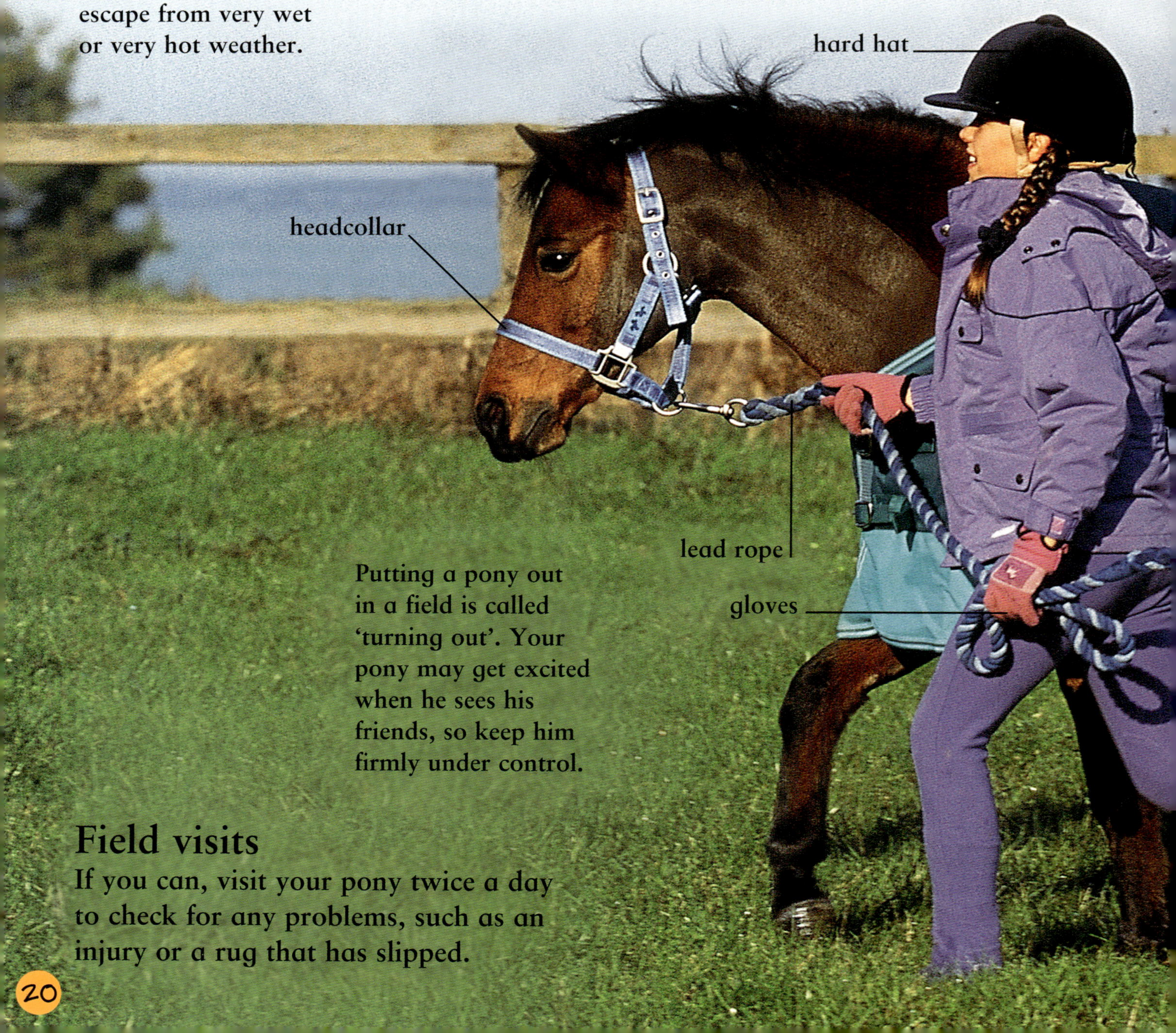


Putting a pony out in a field is called 'turning out'. Your pony may get excited when he sees his friends, so keep him firmly under control.

## Field visits

If you can, visit your pony twice a day to check for any problems, such as an injury or a rug that has slipped.

## Safety first!

If you have to remove poisonous plants from your pony's field, always wear gloves to protect your skin.

Ragwort is very poisonous to ponies. It must be dug or pulled out, then burned by an adult.

Your pony's field needs a supply of fresh water. A trough linked to a water pipe is best.

To help your pony avoid getting worms, remove droppings in a skip or wheelbarrow as often as you can.

Top tip

## Locked up

Check fences, gates and locks often to make sure that they are secure and that your pony cannot get out.

# Clean and tidy

Grooming keeps a pony's skin clean and healthy by removing dried sweat and loose hair. It also makes him look smart. Groom a stabled pony every day, but groom a pony that lives in a field less because the grease and dirt in his coat will help to keep him dry and warm.

In cold weather, keep your pony warm by covering half of him with a rug or blanket while you groom his other half.

1 Carefully remove patches of dirt and sweat with a dandy brush. Never use this stiff brush on your pony's head or tummy.

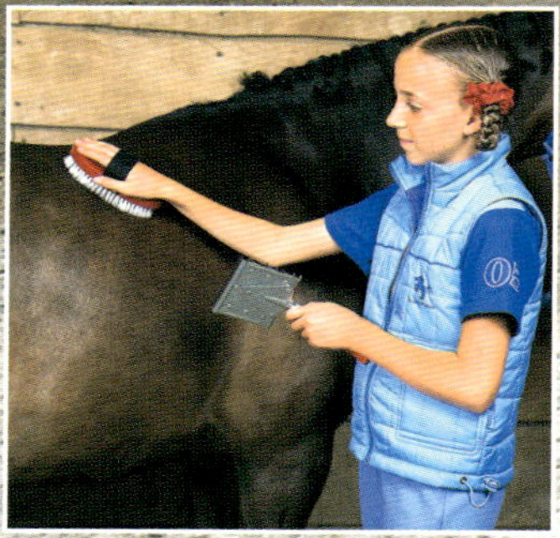

2 Use the soft body brush to groom the whole pony. Start just behind his ears and work towards his tail. Clean the bristles on a curry comb.

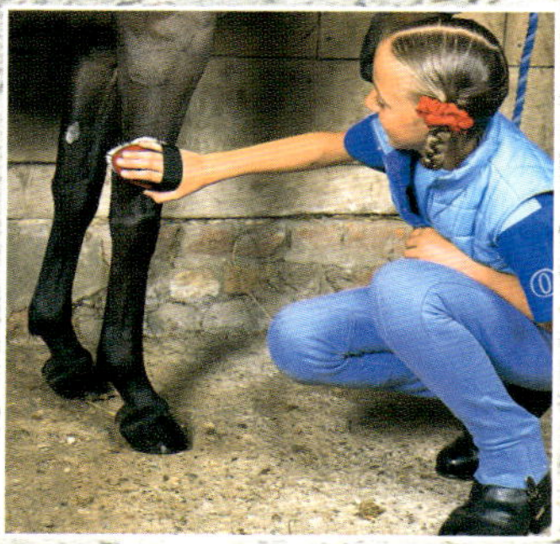

3 Don't stand behind your pony's legs when you groom them. Keep to one side and take care not to knock the bony parts.

4 When you brush your pony's tail, stand to the side of him, not right behind him, in case he kicks out.

## Safety first!

Before you start to groom, always tie up your pony with a headcollar and rope.

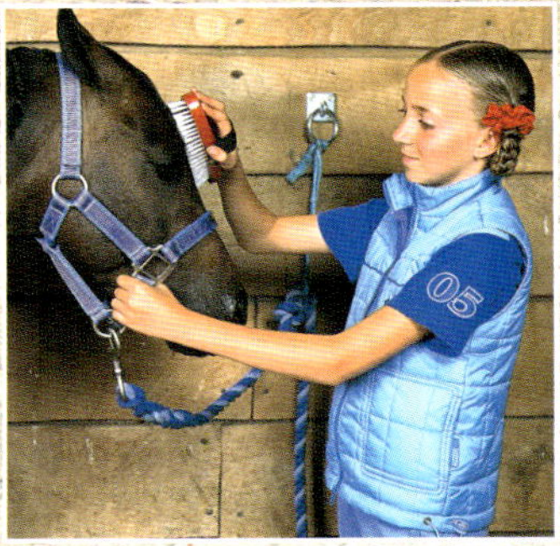

5 Lastly, brush his head with the body brush. Be gentle and keep the bristles away from his eyes.

Top tip

## Face sponge

Wipe around a pony's eyes and nose with a damp sponge. Use a different sponge to clean under his tail.

# Manes and tails

A tidy mane and tail make a pony look extra smart. This is important for a show. A neat mane is easier to plait than a bushy, untidy one. It is easy to spoil a mane by not pulling it correctly, so this job should be done by an older person.

This rider is using a mane comb to comb back a section of hair. Then she pulls out the hairs that are left in the fingers of her other hand.

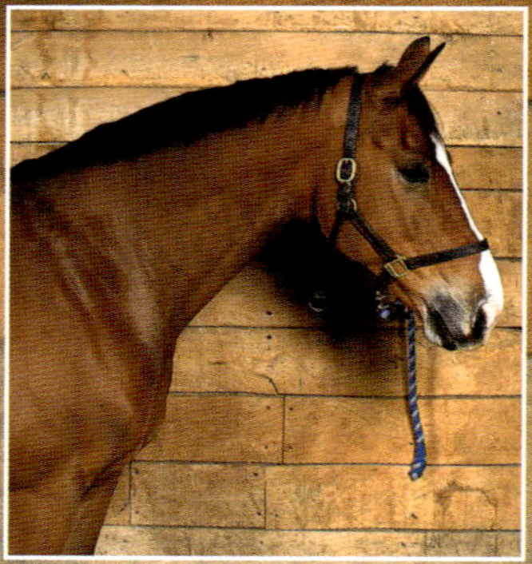

This finished mane has been dampened with a water-brush to help the hairs lie flat.

## Pulling the mane

A pony's mane is thinned and shortened by pulling out some of the hair from the underneath, using the fingers and a metal mane-pulling comb.

## Trimming the tail

Most ponies look best with their tails cut neatly to make a level, straight edge. The tail should hang between their hocks and their fetlocks. A very long tail will become muddy in winter.

Top tip

### Levelling

Round-ended scissors are always used to level off the ends of the pony's tail hairs.

# Clipping

Most ponies grow a thick coat in winter, but this makes them sweaty and uncomfortable when they work. This is why a working pony usually has part of his coat clipped by an experienced person.

Clipping a pony alone is difficult and even dangerous. A helper must always be present to keep the pony calm and to fetch help if there is an accident.

A pony that is doing medium work has a 'trace clip'. Hair is clipped from part of his body and the underside of his neck.

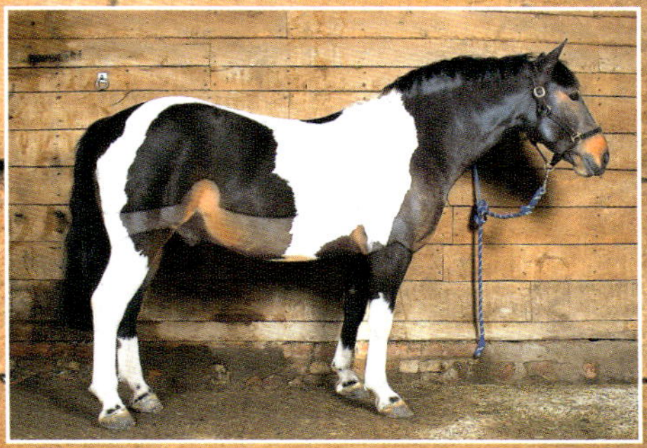

A stabled pony that is doing medium to hard work has a 'blanket clip'. The hair is removed from part of his body and all of his neck.

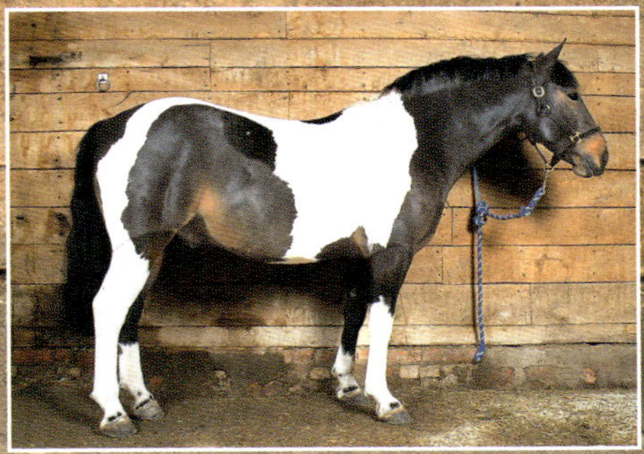

A stabled pony doing hard work is given a 'hunter clip'. The hair is clipped from all of his body and neck, except for a patch under the saddle.

The clippers are used in the opposite direction to the way the pony's coat lies.

## Safety first!

A pony may get very scared when the clippers are near his head. If this happens, it is best to leave the head unclipped.

# Bathtime

Grooming usually keeps a pony clean, but sometimes – such as before a show – he may need bathing with a gentle shampoo. Grey ponies usually have to be bathed more often, but be careful not to overdo it. Too much washing will make the pony's skin and coat dry.

**1** Start washing at your pony's neck and work down the front and sides of his body. Give the mane a good wash too.

Watch what you wear – you may get wet!

Fit your pony with a headcollar so that a helper can hold him.

Your pony will be more comfortable if you use lukewarm water, not cold.

Top tip

## Tail spin

To dry your pony's tail more quickly, swish it around to remove the water.

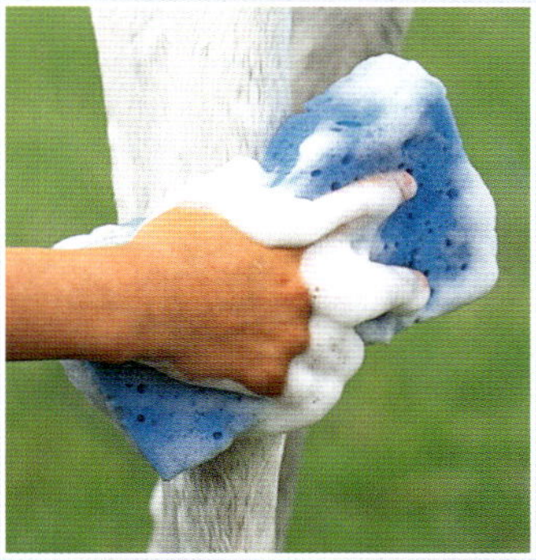

**2** Be very gentle when you sponge the pony's face. Do not let water and shampoo get into his eyes or ears.

**3** Carefully sponge the legs. To wash the hind legs, stand at the pony's side, not behind him, in case he tries to kick.

**4** Wash the tail by dipping it in a bucket of lukewarm water and then rubbing in shampoo. Rinse it thoroughly.

**5** Rinse the pony all over with clean water. Then use a sweat scraper to remove water from his neck and body.

**6** Gently comb the mane. Be careful not to break the hair.

**7** Walk the pony about until he is completely dry.

### Safety first!

Never give a pony a bath on a cold day because he may catch a chill.

### Outdoor rugs

Have your pony measured to make sure his rug fits him. It should be snug but not too tight. Check the rug every day to make sure it is not causing any sore patches.

The ends of the straps are tucked neatly through the keepers.

The rug covers the pony's body down to his elbows.

# Rugs

Rugs protect ponies from the cold and wet, and help to keep them clean. There are waterproof rugs for outdoors, and stable rugs and blankets for ponies that live inside. Thermal rugs dry off a sweaty pony, and light summer sheets help to keep away flies.

Two straps called 'surcingles' fasten underneath the pony. They keep the rug in place even if he gallops or rolls.

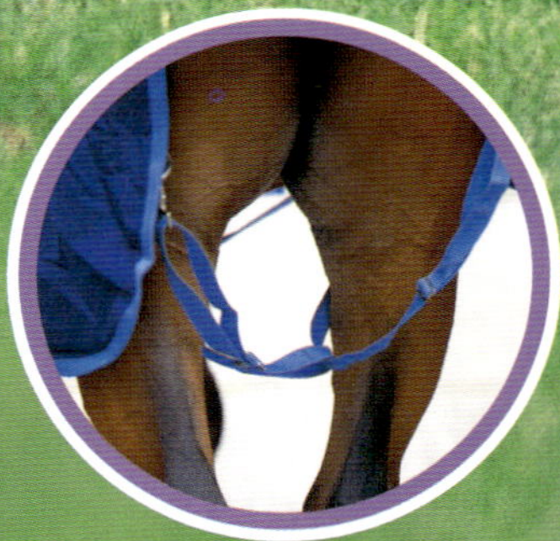

Leg straps are fastened loosely around the pony's hind legs to stop the wind from blowing the rug up.

## Indoor rugs

These are made for stabled ponies and are less heavy than outdoor rugs. If your pony is clipped, he will need to wear a rug for extra warmth, especially at night.

Top tip

### Clean rug

Keep your rugs clean by brushing and washing them. Some can go in a washing machine.

## Putting on a rug

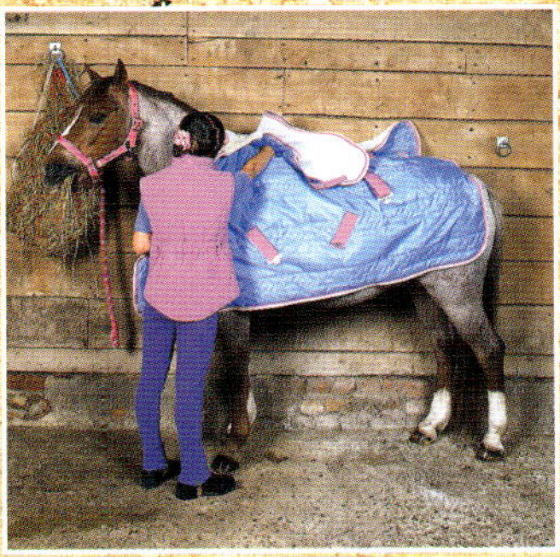

1 Place the rug across your pony's back, well in front of his withers. Do not let the surcingles flap about.

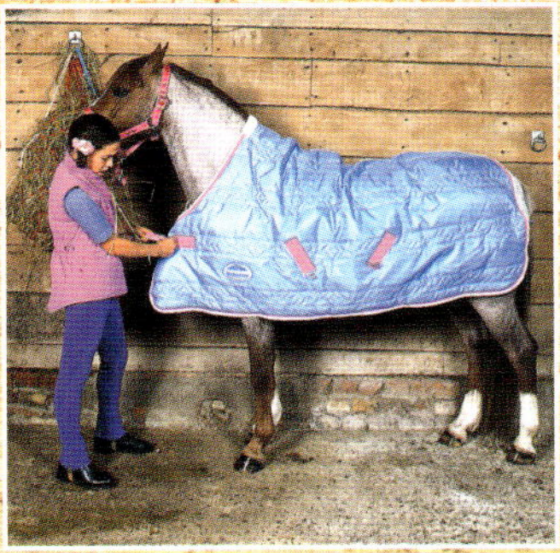

2 Slide the rug back slightly so that it is snugly in place around his neck. Then fasten the front straps.

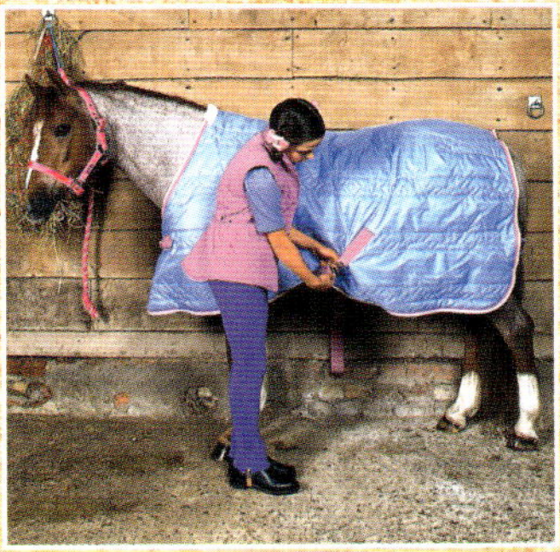

3 Fasten the rug's surcingles under the pony's belly. Take care not to pull the rug forwards over his coat.

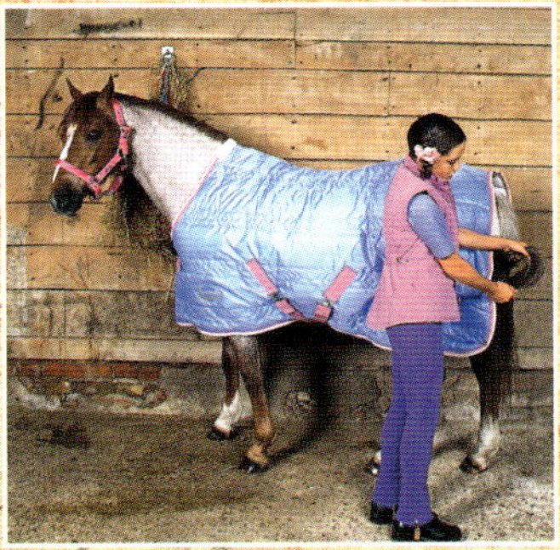

4 Lift his tail over the rear strap, or 'fillet string'. This helps keep the rug in place. Speak to your pony to keep him calm.

# Bandages

Sometimes a pony's legs need to be bandaged for extra protection – when you are taking him in a trailer to a show or if he has an injury, for example. Bandages should be put on only by an experienced older person.

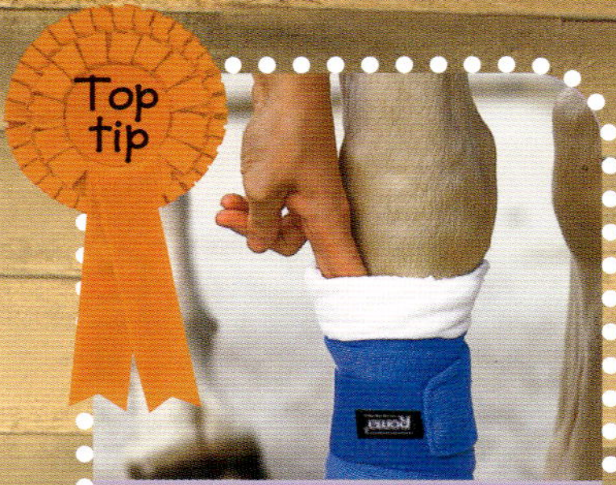


### Finger test

Slide a finger between the pony's leg and the bandage to check it is not too tight.

## Stable bandages

**These are wide bandages that help to keep a pony warm in his stable. They must not be too tight.**

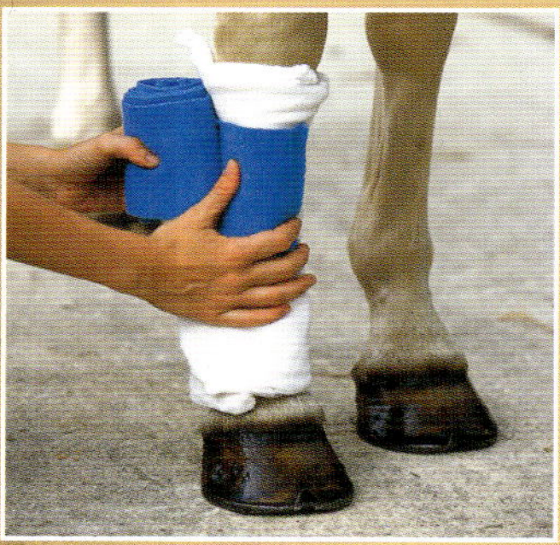

**1** The pony's leg is wrapped in a layer of padding. The stable bandage is wound down the leg from just below the knee.

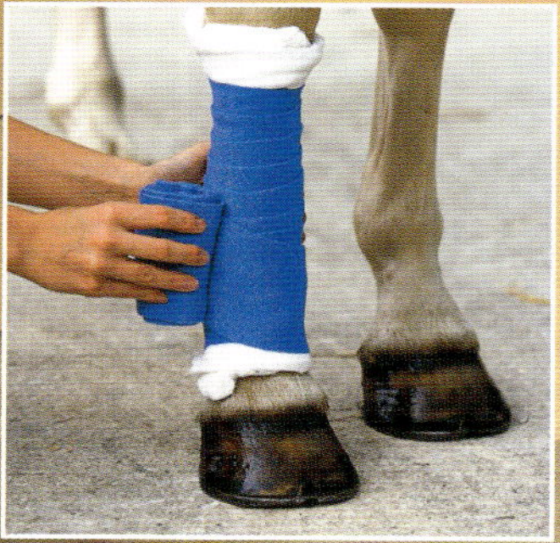

**2** With an even pressure, the pony's leg is bandaged down to the fetlock joint and then up again.

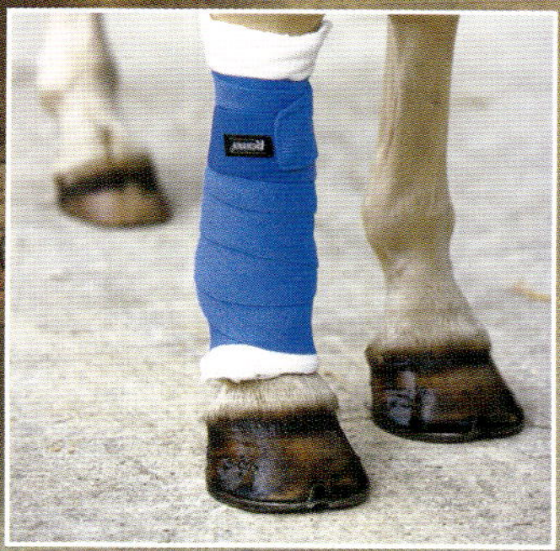

**3** The stable bandage is fastened neatly on the outside of the leg, never at the back or the front.

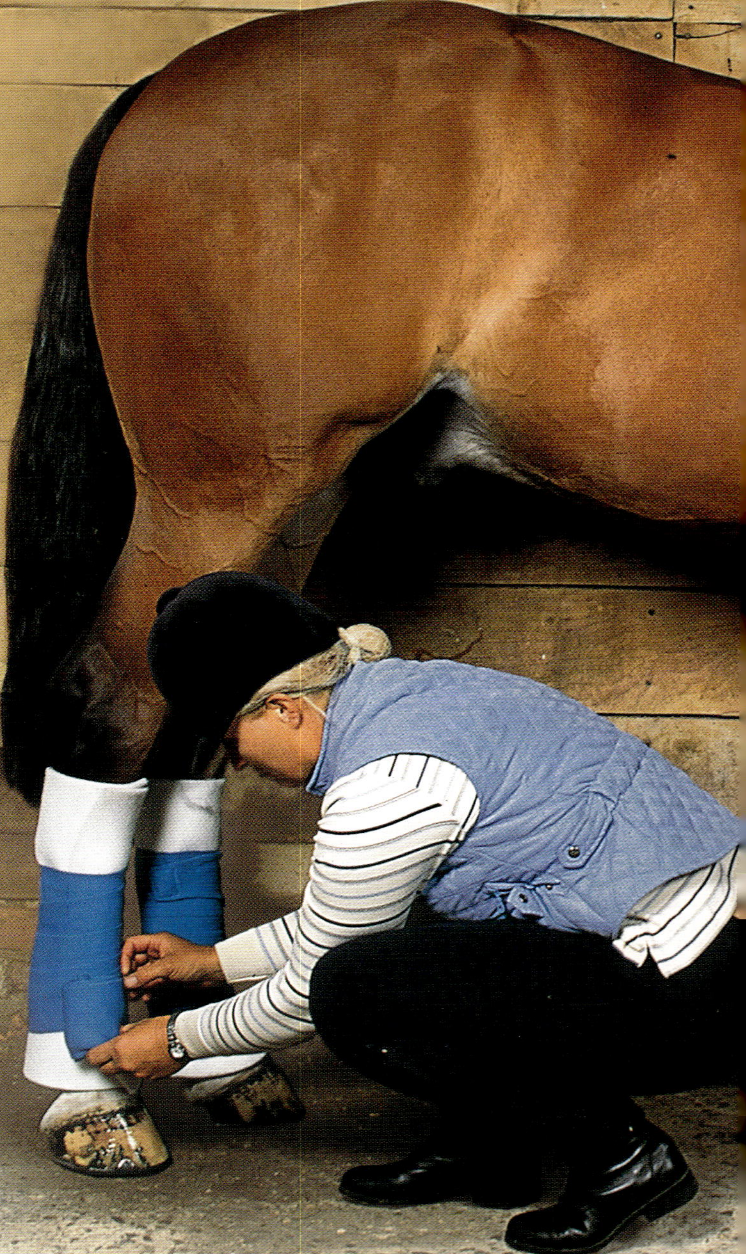

## Tail bandages

A tail bandage keeps the hair at the top of a pony's tail flat and tidy when he is travelling in a trailer. It also stops the tail from being rubbed. It takes practice to bandage a tail correctly, and an adult should check your work carefully.

### Safety first!

Never leave a tail bandage on for more than a few hours, or your pony will become uncomfortable.

1 Pass the end of the bandage under the 'dock', or top of your pony's tail.

2 Wrap the bandage evenly around and down the pony's tail.

3 Finish just above the end of the dock. Tie the tapes in a bow, not too tightly.

Always tie up your pony when he is being bandaged.

Bandages should be washed often, and rolled up tightly so they are ready to be re-used.

Bandages are put over a layer of padding, such as gamgee tissue.

# Boots and shoes

When a pony carries a rider, his legs and feet need special care. Boots protect the legs from injury. Shoes stop the horn part of the hoof from wearing down too quickly and making the pony's feet sore.

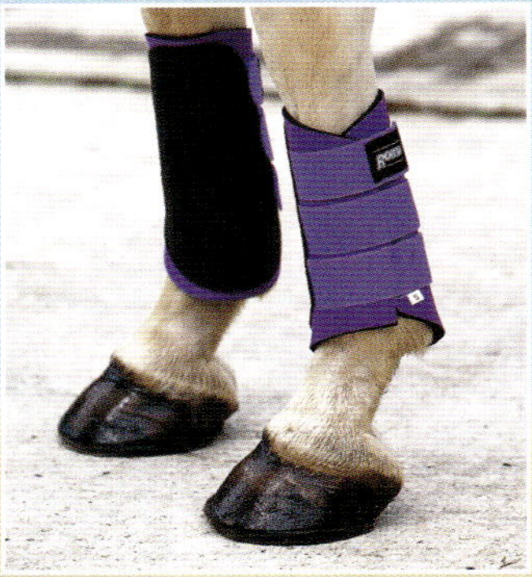

'Exercise boots' are worn on all four legs. They help to prevent injuries, especially if the pony knocks one of his legs against the opposite one.

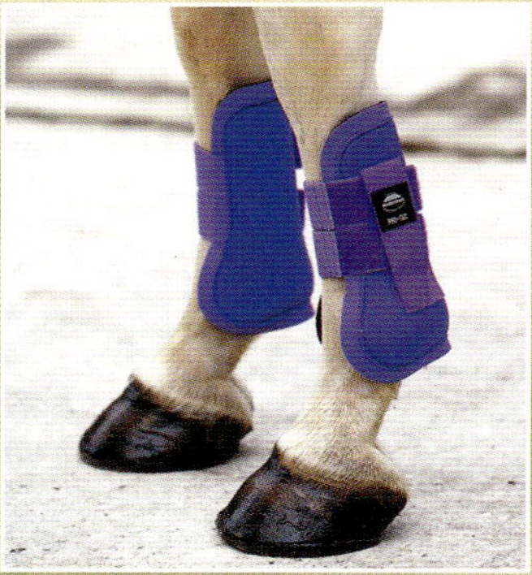

'Tendon boots' protect the backs of a pony's forelegs from being hit by the toes of his hind feet. The boots in this picture have an open front.

'Overreach boots' are worn on the forelegs. They protect the heels of the forelegs from knocks by the toes of the hind feet.

# Shoeing a pony

A pony with strong feet that is not doing much work may not need shoes. But most ridden ponies wear shoes to protect their feet. The horn of their feet grows all the time, so the shoes must be taken off and the feet trimmed regularly by a farrier.

## Safety first!

Check your pony's hooves for cracks. They could be a sign that he has a foot problem.

1 The farrier will probably need to trim your pony's feet every six weeks, but this depends on how fast your pony's feet grow.

2 Shoes are shaped from hot iron, using a hammer and an anvil. Hot shoes give a better fit than cold ones.

3 The farrier holds the hot shoe on the hoof to test the fit. It does not hurt the pony because the outer part of his foot does not feel anything.

4 The shoe is nailed into place. The farrier takes care not to drive the nails into the sensitive inner part of the foot.

# A healthy pony

Ponies are quite tough animals, but they often pick up injuries, especially in fields. Try to check your pony every day for cuts, lumps or skin problems. A good time to do this is when you are grooming him. If you are not sure about anything, ask an adult to call the vet.

The vet will watch your pony trot to see if his shoulder, leg or foot is hurting.

Keep a first-aid box handy. Inside the box put wound powder, sterile dressings, bandages, cotton wool, poultices and a pair of curved scissors.

## Lameness

This pony is lame, which means that he cannot walk properly and must not be ridden. The vet is checking the injured leg.

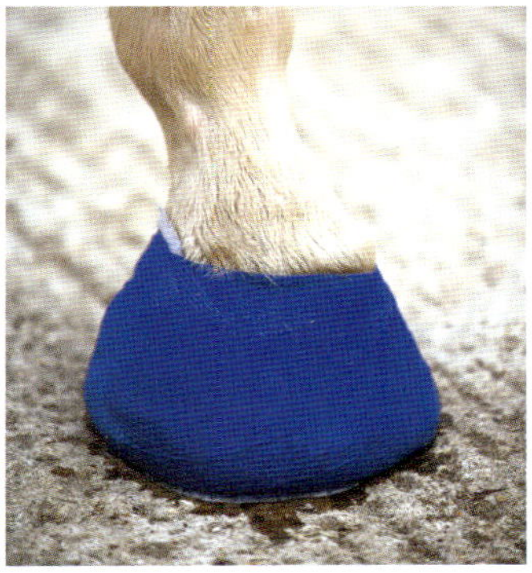

A 'poultice' is a soft pad made from cotton wool that helps to draw dirt or pus from a wound. This foot poultice is kept in place with a bandage.

Mud fever is a skin infection that affects ponies in very wet weather. Watch out for matted hair and scabs around the heels. It must be treated by a vet.

## Safety first!

Tetanus is a disease that is caused by germs that live in the soil. To protect your pony from tetanus, he must be given a vaccine, or injection, by a vet.

Top tip

## Walk out

Sometimes it helps a lame pony to have a short walk each day. Choose a quiet place and always lead him with a bridle.

# Cleaning tack

Tack is riding equipment, such as saddles, stirrup irons and bridles. It should be cleaned every time it is used. Use a damp sponge to wash off grease and dirt, and saddle soap to keep leather soft.

## The saddle

**Remove the stirrups and girth and clean them separately. Sponge over the whole saddle, including underneath. Check the stitching and buckles for signs of wear.**

Do not put too much soap on the saddle seat.

Wash any mud off the stirrup irons and dry them with a clean cloth. Metal polish will make them look extra smart.

A 'numnah' is a pad that keeps the saddle clean. Brush its underside after every use and wash it often with mild soap powder.

## The bridle

After every ride, sponge clean and then dry the bit. The best way to clean the whole bridle is to take it apart.

1 With a damp sponge, clean off all the grease and dirt. Do not wet the leather as this will make it hard.

2 Rub a small amount of saddle soap into all the straps. From time to time, use a special leather dressing.

3 Put the bridle back together. Fasten all the buckles and studs, and push the ends of the straps through the keepers.

# Tacked up

It is important that your pony's tack fits correctly. The bit must be the right size for his mouth. The straps of the bridle must be carefully adjusted to fit your pony's head comfortably. All ponies are a different shape, so it is best if each one has his own saddle.

## Safety first!

Before you mount, check that the girth is tight enough to stop the saddle slipping.

## Lead-rein riding

The safest way to begin riding is on a lead rein. The leader walks or jogs beside the pony, keeping him under control, while you learn how to sit in the saddle and how to hold and use the reins. The leader should be an older, experienced person.

Learning to trot is best done on the lead rein. You may need to hold the front of the saddle to begin with. Never pull on the reins to keep your balance.

The throatlash must not be too tight.

The noseband sits well above the pony's nostrils.

The stirrup iron is fixed to the saddle by a leather strap. This safety iron has an elastic side that allows your foot to slide out if you fall off.

Top tip

### Lungeing

Sending a pony round in circles on the end of a long rein is called 'lungeing'. Riding on the lunge without reins will help you learn to balance in the saddle.

# Ready to go out

Before you go out for a ride, check that your tack is in good condition. Always wear proper riding clothes. If you are going on the roads, you must make sure that other road users can see you well.

## Safety first!

Always go out with an older, more experienced rider. Never ride on the roads in foggy weather or at dusk.

Stirrups are the right length when your finger is on the stirrup leather buckle and the bottom of the iron reaches your armpit.

When you are in the saddle, you may have to tighten the girth by one more hole.

In cold weather, your pony may need to wear an exercise sheet. Choose one with reflective strips.

Brushing boots stop your pony knocking his foot against the inside of the opposite leg.

A correctly fitted riding hat is the most important piece of your equipment.

Wear a 'tabard' with reflective strips on the front and back.

Wear gloves to give you a better grip on the reins.

Always wear proper riding boots, never trainers or wellingtons.

Top tip

## Phone home

Take your mobile phone with you so you can call for help if you have a problem.

Always check that your tack is properly fitted before you go out. Never use a bridle or saddle with worn stitching.

## Warming up and down

Do not start trotting or cantering as soon as you set off. First, walk your pony for a while to loosen up his muscles. When you go home, especially after a fast ride, always walk the last kilometre or two. Your pony should be cool and not out of breath when he reaches his stable.

To turn left or right, hold your arm out straight, with a flat palm facing the front.

To ask a car in front of you to stop, raise your hand with the palm facing forwards.

To ask a car behind you to drive past, move your hand in a forward movement, with your arm straight.

# Riding safely

Ride on roads only if your pony is not scared of traffic. Stay alert at all times, because something other than vehicles – a bird or a barking dog – might scare your pony. You need to learn how to make signals to other road users. Practise these at home.

Top tip

## Thank you

After you make a signal, look at the driver and say thank you by smiling and nodding your head.

Hold both reins (and your whip if you have one) in one hand.

Make sure you open the gate far enough for the pony to walk through without knocking himself on the post.

## Gates

Being able to open and shut a gate without dismounting is very useful when you go for a ride in the country. Practise riding the pony around the gate and through the gap. Most ponies soon understand how it is done.

Always close the gate securely behind you to stop any farm animals from getting out of their field.

# Galloping

One of the most exciting things you can do with your pony is to go for a gallop. You must be a good, confident rider.

## Fast riding

Remember that ponies love to gallop too. They can become quite excited, especially when they are heading home! Make sure that the owners of the land do not mind if you gallop your pony in their field.

Top tip

### Hometime

If you walk the last kilometre back to the stables, your pony will arrive home cool and relaxed. Groom him and then put on his rug before you feed him.

### Safety first!

If you gallop with other riders, leave plenty of room between each pony.

# Glossary

**Breed**
A horse or pony group that has been bred carefully over a period of time. Pony breeds include the Connemara, the Welsh and the Caspian.

**Chaff**
This is chopped hay, or a mixture of hay and oat straw. It adds bulk to a stabled pony's feed and encourages greedy ponies to eat more slowly.

**Coarse mix**
Vitamins and minerals are usually added to this all-in-one feed.

**Colic**
This is a stomach pain, often caused by eating too much or by a sudden change in diet. A pony that has colic may sweat and repeatedly roll on the ground.

**Curry comb**
A grooming tool made of metal, rubber or plastic. A metal curry comb is used to clean the body brush. A rubber or plastic curry comb is used to remove mud from the pony's coat.

**Farrier**
A person who trims a pony's feet, and makes and fits his shoes. Another word for a farrier is blacksmith.

**Hands**
Traditionally, horses and ponies are measured in hands. One hand equals 10 centimetres, which is roughly the width of an adult's hand.

**Haylage**
Wilted grass is used to make this type of roughage. It is sealed in plastic wrapping.

**Horn**
The wall of a pony's hoof is made of horn, which, like our fingernails, keeps on growing and does not feel pain when trimmed.

**Lame**
When a pony has hurt his foot or leg, and cannot walk properly.

**Laminitis**
If a pony eats too much rich food or has too little exercise, the inside parts of his hoof can swell up. This is known as laminitis.

**Livery**
Paying to keep your pony at someone else's yard is called livery. It will cost less if you do some of the work, such as mucking out.

**Pony cubes**
A type of feed that has been ground up, steamed and then shaped into nuts or cubes.

**Thrush**
This foot infection is usually caused by standing in wet bedding. The pony's foot begins to rot and smells bad.

**Vet (short for veterinary surgeon)**
A highly trained person who looks after the health of animals.

**Withers**
The top of a pony's shoulders, between the neck and the back.

**Worms**
These harmful parasites live inside horses and ponies. To control the problem, you need to treat your pony with special powders or pastes.

# Index

# Acknowledgements


The publisher would like to thank the following for their help in the production of this book:

Models: Alexis, Amy, Charley, Charlotte, Ciara, Elliot, Fraser, Harry, Hollie, India, Justice, Leanne, Lucy, Raija, Rhianna and Simi

Ponies: Cracker, Denzel, Jasper, Pickwick, Pie, Rosie, Scamp, Big Scamp, Teddy and Tiger

Lisa Benton and Pat Seager

The Justine Armstrong-Small team (www.armstrong-small.co.uk):
Justine and Hazel Armstrong-Small
Grooms: Becky, Katie, Lisa and Vicky

Jason Robertson, registered farrier

Harolds Park Farm Riding Centre

Cuddly Ponies, Dublin Clothing and Roma (www.dublinclothing.com)

Photography: Matthew Roberts (www.matthewrobertsphotographer.com)

All photographs by Matthew Roberts with the exception of: page 8cl, 8bl, 9bl, 14bl, 15cr, 15br, 37tr (Bob Langrish, www.boblangrish.co.uk)